2013

I0441212

Status of the Social Security and Medicare Programs

A SUMMARY OF THE 2013 ANNUAL REPORTS

Social Security and Medicare
Boards of Trustees

A MESSAGE TO THE PUBLIC:

Each year the Trustees of the Social Security and Medicare trust funds report on the current and projected financial status of the two programs. This message summarizes the 2013 Annual Reports.

Neither Medicare nor Social Security can sustain projected long-run programs in full under currently scheduled financing, and legislative changes are necessary to avoid disruptive consequences for beneficiaries and taxpayers. If lawmakers take action sooner rather than later, more options and more time will be available to phase in changes so that the public has adequate time to prepare. Earlier action will also help elected officials minimize adverse impacts on vulnerable populations, including lower-income workers and people already dependent on program benefits.

Social Security and Medicare together accounted for 38 percent of federal expenditures in fiscal year 2012. Both programs will experience cost growth substantially in excess of GDP growth through the mid-2030s due to rapid population aging caused by the large baby-boom generation entering retirement and lower-birth-rate generations entering employment and, in the case of Medicare, to growth in expenditures per beneficiary exceeding growth in per capita GDP. In later years, projected costs expressed as a share of GDP trend up slowly for Medicare and are relatively flat for Social Security, reflecting very gradual population aging caused by increasing longevity and slower growth in per-beneficiary health care costs.

Social Security

Social Security's Disability Insurance (DI) program satisfies neither the Trustees' long-range test of close actuarial balance nor their short-range test of financial adequacy and faces the most immediate financing shortfall of any of the separate trust funds. DI Trust Fund reserves expressed as a percent of annual cost (the trust fund ratio) declined to 85 percent at the beginning of 2013, and the Trustees project trust fund depletion in 2016, the same year projected in the last Trustees Report. DI cost has exceeded non-interest income since 2005, and the trust fund ratio has declined since peaking in 2003. While legislation is needed to address all of Social Security's financial imbalances, the need has become most urgent with respect to the program's DI component. Lawmakers need to act soon to avoid reduced payments to DI beneficiaries three years from now.

Social Security's total expenditures have exceeded non-interest income of its combined trust funds since 2010, and the Trustees estimate that Social Security cost will exceed non-interest income throughout the 75-year projection period. The deficit of non-interest income relative to cost was about $49 billion in 2010, $45 billion in 2011, and $55 billion in 2012. The Trustees project that this cash-flow deficit will average about $75 billion between 2013 and 2018 before rising steeply as income growth slows to the sustainable trend rate after the economic recovery is complete and the number of beneficiaries continues to grow at a substantially faster rate than the number of covered workers. Redemption of trust fund asset reserves by the General Fund of the Treasury will provide the resources needed to offset Social Security's annual aggregate cash-flow deficits. Since the cash-flow deficit will be less than interest earnings through 2020, reserves of the combined trust funds measured in current dollars will continue to grow, but not by enough to prevent the ratio of reserves to one year's projected cost (the combined trust fund ratio) from declining. (This ratio peaked in 2008, declined through 2012, and is expected to decline steadily in future years.) After 2020, Treasury will redeem trust fund asset reserves to the extent that program cost exceeds tax revenue and interest earnings until depletion of total trust fund reserves in 2033, the same year projected in last year's Trustees Report. Thereafter, tax income would be sufficient to pay about three-quarters of scheduled benefits through 2087.

A temporary reduction in the Social Security payroll tax rate in 2011 and 2012 reduced payroll tax revenues by an estimated $222 billion in total. The legislation establishing the payroll tax reduction also provided for transfers from the General Fund to the trust funds in order to "replicate to the extent possible" payments that would have occurred if the payroll tax reduction had not been enacted. Those General Fund reimbursements amounted to about 15 percent of the program's non-interest income in 2011 and 2012. The temporary payroll tax reduction expired at the end of 2012.

Under current projections, the annual cost of Social Security benefits expressed as a share of workers' taxable earnings will grow rapidly from 11.3 percent in 2007, the last pre-recession year, to roughly 17.0 percent in 2037, and will then decline slightly before slowly increasing after 2050. Cost displays a slightly different pattern when expressed as a share of GDP. Program cost equaled 4.2 percent of GDP in 2007, the last pre-recession year, and the Trustees project that cost will increase to 6.2 percent of GDP for 2036, then decline to about 6.0 percent of GDP by 2050, and thereafter rise slowly reaching 6.2 percent by 2087.

The projected 75-year actuarial deficit for the combined Old-Age and Survivors Insurance and Disability Insurance (OASDI) Trust Funds is 2.72 percent of taxable payroll, up from 2.67 percent projected in last year's report. This deficit amounts to 21 percent of program non-interest income or 17 percent of program cost. A 0.06 percentage point increase in the OASDI actuarial deficit would have been expected if nothing had changed other than the one-year extension of the valuation period to 2087. The effects of recently enacted legislation, updated demographic data, updated economic data and assumptions further worsened the actuarial deficit, but these effects were completely offset by the favorable effects of updated programmatic data and improved methodologies.

While the combined OASDI program fails the long-range test of close actuarial balance, it does satisfy the test for short-range (ten-year) financial adequacy. The Trustees project that the combined trust fund asset reserves at the beginning of each year will exceed that year's projected cost through 2027.

Medicare

The Trustees project that the Medicare Hospital Insurance (HI) Trust Fund will be the next to face depletion after the DI Trust Fund. The projected date of HI Trust Fund depletion is 2026, two years later than projected in last year's report, at which time dedicated revenues would be sufficient to pay 87 percent of HI cost. The Trustees project that the share of HI cost that can be financed with HI dedicated revenues will decline slowly to 71 percent in 2047, and then rise slowly until it reaches 73 percent in 2087. As it has since 2008, the HI Trust Fund will pay out more in hospital benefits and other expenditures than it receives in income in all years until reserve depletion.

The projected HI Trust Fund's long-term actuarial imbalance is smaller than that of the combined Social Security trust funds under the assumptions employed in this report.

The estimated 75-year actuarial deficit in the HI Trust Fund is 1.11 percent of taxable payroll, down from 1.35 percent projected in last year's report. The HI fund again fails the test of short-range financial adequacy, as its trust fund ratio is already below 100 percent and is expected to decline continuously until reserve depletion in 2026. The fund also continues to fail the long-range test of close actuarial balance. The HI 75-year actuarial imbalance amounts to 29 percent of tax receipts or 23 percent of program cost.

The modest improvement in the outlook for HI long-term finances is principally due to: (i) lower projected spending for most HI service categories—especially for skilled nursing facilities—to reflect lower-than-expected spending in 2012 and other recent data; (ii) lower projected Medicare Advantage program costs that reflect recent data suggesting that certain provisions of the Affordable Care Act will reduce growth in these costs by more than was previously projected; and (iii) a refinement in projection methods that reduces assumed per beneficiary cost growth during the transition period between the short-range projections and the long-range projections. Partially offsetting these favorable changes to the projections are somewhat lower projected levels of tax income that reflect lower-than-expected tax income in 2012.

The Trustees project that Part B of Supplementary Medical Insurance (SMI), which pays doctors' bills and other outpatient expenses, and Part D of SMI, which provides access to prescription drug coverage, will remain adequately financed into the indefinite future because current law automatically provides financing each year to meet the next year's expected costs. However, the aging population and rising health care costs cause SMI projected costs to grow steadily from 2.0 percent of GDP in 2012 to approximately 3.3 percent of GDP in 2035, and then more slowly to 4.0 percent of GDP by 2087. General revenues will finance roughly three quarters of these costs, and premiums paid by beneficiaries almost all of the remaining quarter. SMI also receives a small amount of financing from special payments by States and from fees on manufacturers and importers of brand-name prescription drugs. Projected costs for

Part B assume an almost 25-percent reduction in Medicare payment rates for physician services will be implemented in 2014 as required by current law, which is highly unlikely.

The Trustees project that total Medicare cost (including both HI and SMI expenditures) will grow from approximately 3.6 percent of GDP in 2012 to 5.6 percent of GDP by 2035, and will increase gradually thereafter to about 6.5 percent of GDP by 2087.

The drawdown of Social Security and HI Trust Fund reserves and the general revenue transfers into SMI will result in mounting pressure on the Federal budget. In fact, pressure is already evident. For the seventh consecutive year, the Social Security Act requires that the Trustees issue a "Medicare funding warning" because projected non-dedicated sources of revenues—primarily general revenues—are expected to continue to account for more than 45 percent of Medicare's outlays in 2013, a threshold breached for the first time in fiscal year 2010.

Conclusion

Lawmakers should address the financial challenges facing Social Security and Medicare as soon as possible. Taking action sooner rather than later will leave more options and more time available to phase in changes so that the public has adequate time to prepare.

By the Trustees:

JACOB J. LEW,
Secretary of the Treasury,
and Managing Trustee
of the Trust Funds.

SETH D. HARRIS,
Acting Secretary of Labor,
and Trustee.

KATHLEEN SEBELIUS,
Secretary of Health
and Human Services,
and Trustee.

CAROLYN W. COLVIN,
Acting Commissioner
of Social Security,
and Trustee.

CHARLES P. BLAHOUS III,
Trustee.

ROBERT D. REISCHAUER,
Trustee.

A SUMMARY OF THE 2013 ANNUAL SOCIAL SECURITY AND MEDICARE TRUST FUND REPORTS

Projected long-range costs for both Medicare and Social Security are not sustainable with currently scheduled financing and will require legislative action to avoid disruptive consequences for beneficiaries and taxpayers. If lawmakers act sooner rather than later, they can consider more options and more time will be available to phase in the changes, giving the public adequate time to prepare. Earlier action would also provide more opportunity to ameliorate any adverse impacts on vulnerable populations, including lower-income workers and people already dependent on program benefits.

What Are the Trust Funds? Congress established trust funds managed by the Secretary of the Treasury to account for Social Security and Medicare income and disbursements. The Treasury credits Social Security and Medicare taxes, premiums, and other income to the funds. There are four separate trust funds. For Social Security, the Old-Age and Survivors Insurance (OASI) Trust Fund pays retirement and survivors benefits and the Disability Insurance (DI) Trust Fund pays disability benefits. (OASDI is the designation for the two trust funds when they are considered on a combined basis.) For Medicare, the Hospital Insurance (HI) Trust Fund pays for inpatient hospital and related care. The Supplementary Medical Insurance (SMI) Trust Fund comprises two separate accounts: Part B, which pays for physician and outpatient services, and Part D, which covers the prescription drug benefit. In 2012, 45.9 million people received OASI benefits, 10.9 million received DI benefits, and 50.7 million were covered under Medicare.

The only disbursements permitted from the funds are benefit payments and administrative costs. Federal law requires that all excess funds be invested in interest-bearing securities backed by the full faith and credit of the United States. The Department of the Treasury currently invests all program revenues in special non-marketable securities of the U.S. Government which earn a market rate of interest. The balances in the trust funds represent the accumulated value, including interest, of all prior program annual surpluses and deficits, and provide automatic authority to pay benefits.

What Were the Trust Fund Results in 2012? Trust fund operations, in billions of dollars, are shown in the following table. (Totals may not add due to rounding.) The OASI Trust Fund showed a net increase in asset reserves in 2012; reserves in the DI, HI, and SMI Trust Funds declined.

	OASI	DI	HI	SMI
Reserves (end of 2011)	$2,524.1	$153.9	$244.2	$80.7
Income during 2012	731.1	109.1	243.0	293.9
Cost during 2012.	645.5	140.3	266.8	307.4
Net change in reserves	85.6	-31.2	-23.8	-13.5
Reserves (end of 2012)	2,609.7	122.7	220.4	67.2

The following table shows payments, by category, from each trust fund in 2012. (Totals may not add due to rounding.)

Category *(in billions)*	OASI	DI	HI	SMI
Benefit payments	$637.9	$136.9	$262.9	$303.0
Railroad Retirement financial interchange	4.1	0.5	—	—
Administrative expenses	3.4	2.9	3.9	4.4
Total	645.5	140.3	266.8	307.4

Trust fund income, by source, in 2012 is shown below. (Totals may not add due to rounding.)

Source *(in billions)*	OASI	DI	HI	SMI
Payroll taxes	$503.9	$85.6	$205.7	—
Taxes on OASDI benefits	26.7	0.6	18.6	—
Beneficiary premiums	—	—	3.7	$66.6
Transfers from States.	—	—	—	8.4
General Fund reimbursements . .	97.7	16.5	0.5	—
General revenues.	—	—	—	214.0
Interest earnings	102.8	6.4	10.6	2.8
Other	a	—	3.9	2.2
Total.	731.1	109.1	243.0	293.9

a Less than $50 million.

In 2012, Social Security's cost continued to exceed the program's tax income and also continued to exceed its non-interest income, a trend that the Trustees project to continue throughout the short-range period (2013-22) and beyond. The 2012 deficit of tax income relative to cost was $169 billion. The temporary 2-percentage point reduction in the 2012 OASDI employee payroll tax rate, for which the trust funds were fully reimbursed by the General Fund, accounts for $114 billion of the 2012 deficit.

In 2012, the HI fund used interest income ($11 billion) and asset reserves ($24 billion) to help finance expenditures beyond those that could have been made solely on the basis of tax and premium income. For SMI, transfers from the General Fund of the Treasury represent the largest source of income. Because Part B account asset reserves were above the level considered to be adequate at the end of 2011, Part B financing for 2012 was set intentionally to draw down some of the excess reserves, resulting in a decrease of about $13 billion.

What is the Outlook for Future Social Security and Medicare Costs in Relation to GDP? One instructive way to view the projected costs of Social Security and Medicare is to compare the costs of scheduled benefits for the two programs with the gross domestic product (GDP), the most frequently used measure of the total output of the U.S. economy (Chart A). Under the intermediate assumptions employed in the reports and throughout this Summary, costs for both programs increase substantially through 2035 when measured this way because: (1) the number of beneficiaries rises rapidly as the baby-boom generation retires; and (2) the lower birth rates that have persisted since the baby boom cause slower growth of the labor force and GDP. Social Security's projected annual cost increases to about 6.2 percent of GDP by 2035, declines to 6.0 percent by 2050, and remains between 6.0 and 6.2 percent of GDP through 2087. Under current law, projected Medicare cost rises to 5.6 percent of GDP by 2035, largely due to the rapid growth in the number of beneficiaries, and then to 6.5 percent in 2087, with growth in health care cost per beneficiary becoming the larger factor later in the valuation period.

Chart A–Social Security and Medicare Cost as a Percentage of GDP

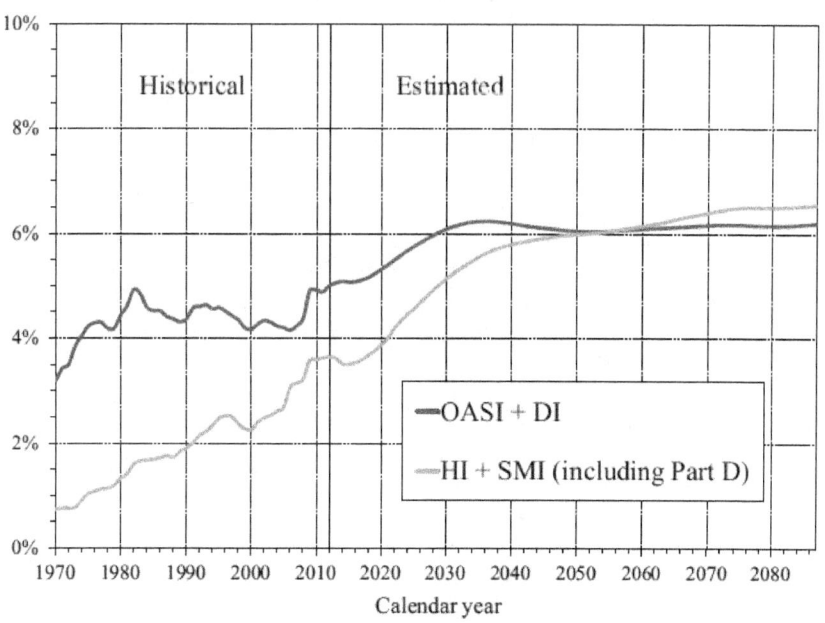

In 2012, the combined cost of the Social Security and Medicare programs equaled 8.7 percent of GDP. The Trustees project an increase to 11.8 percent of GDP in 2035 and 12.7 percent of GDP in 2087. Although Medicare cost (3.6 percent of GDP) is smaller than Social Security cost (5.0 percent of GDP) in 2012, the gap closes gradually until 2056, when Medicare is projected to be the more costly program. During the final decade of the long-range projection period, Medicare cost is modestly larger than Social Security cost.

The projected costs for OASDI and HI depicted in Chart A and elsewhere in this document reflect the full cost of scheduled current-law benefits without regard to whether the trust funds will have sufficient resources to meet these obligations. Current law precludes payment of any benefits beyond the amount that can be financed by the trust funds, that is, from annual income and trust fund reserves. In years after trust fund depletion, the amount of benefits that would be payable is lower than shown, as described later in this summary, because benefit cost exceeds annual income. In addition, the projected costs assume realization of the full estimated savings of the Affordable Care Act as well as adherence to Medicare's sustainable growth rate limits. Lawmakers are likely to prevent an almost 25-percent reduction in payment rates for physician services that would take effect in 2014 under current law. Also, as described in the Medicare Trustees Report, the projections for HI and SMI Part B depend significantly on the sustained effectiveness of various current-law cost-saving measures—in particular, the lower increases in Medicare payment rates to most categories of health care providers.

What is the Outlook for Future Social Security and Medicare HI Costs and Income in Relation to Taxable Earnings? Since the primary source of income for OASDI and HI is the payroll tax, it is informative to express the programs' incomes and costs as percentages of taxable payroll—that is, of the base of worker earnings taxed to support each program (Chart B). Both the OASDI and HI annual cost rates rise over the long run from their 2012 levels (13.79 and 3.67 percent). Projected Social Security cost grows to 16.98 percent of taxable payroll by 2035, declines to 16.78 percent in 2050, and then rises gradually to 18.01 percent in 2087. The projected Medicare HI cost rate rises to 5.44 percent of taxable payroll in 2050, and thereafter gradually increases to 5.87 percent in 2087. HI taxable payroll is almost 25 percent larger than that of OASDI because the HI payroll tax is imposed on all earnings while OASDI taxes apply only to earnings up to an annual maximum ($113,700 in 2013).

The OASDI income rate—which includes payroll taxes, taxes on benefits, and any other transfers of revenues to the trust funds excepting interest payments—was 12.83 percent in 2012 and increases slowly over time, reaching 13.25 percent in 2087. The scheduled payroll tax rate remains unchanged from the current 12.4 percent level. Annual income from the other tax source, the taxation of OASDI benefits, will increase gradually

relative to taxable payroll as a greater proportion of Social Security benefits is subject to taxation in future years, but will continue to be a relatively small component of program income.

**Chart B–OASDI and HI Income and Cost as a Percentage
of Taxable Payroll**

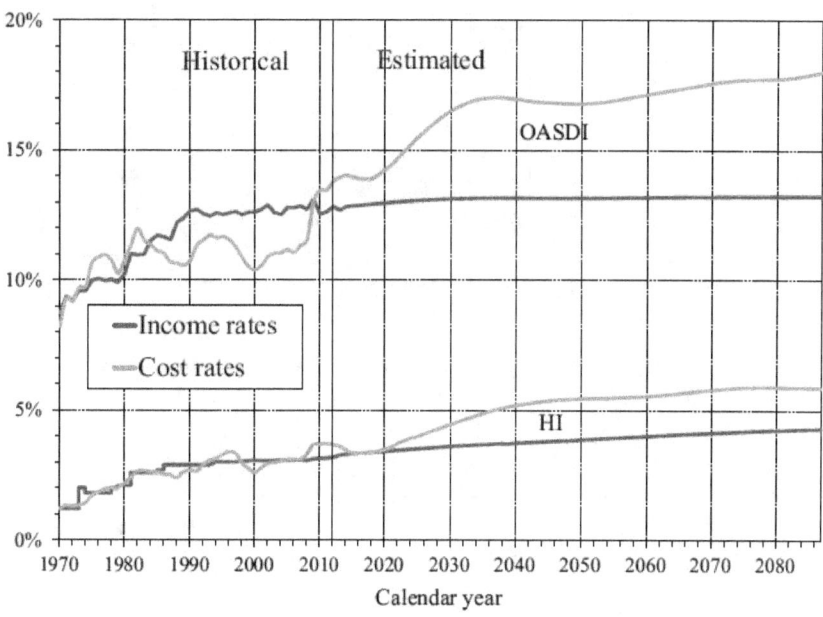

Calendar year

The HI income rate—which includes payroll taxes and taxes on OASDI
benefits, but excludes interest payments—rises gradually from 3.18 percent in 2012 to 4.30 percent in 2087 due to the Affordable Care Act's
increase in payroll tax rates for high earners beginning in 2013. Individual
tax return filers with earnings above $200,000, and joint return filers with
earnings above $250,000, will pay an additional 0.9 percent tax on earn-
ings above these earnings thresholds. An increasing fraction of all earnings will be subject to the higher tax rate over time because the thresholds
are not indexed.

**How Will Cost Growth in the Different Parts of Medicare Change the
Sources of Program Financing?** As Medicare cost grows over time,
general revenue and beneficiary premiums will play an increasing role in
financing the program. Chart C shows scheduled cost and non-interest
revenue sources under current law for HI and SMI combined as a percentage of GDP. The total cost line is the same as displayed in Chart A and
shows Medicare cost rising to 6.5 percent of GDP by 2087.

Chart C–Medicare Cost and Non-Interest Income by Source as a Percentage of GDP

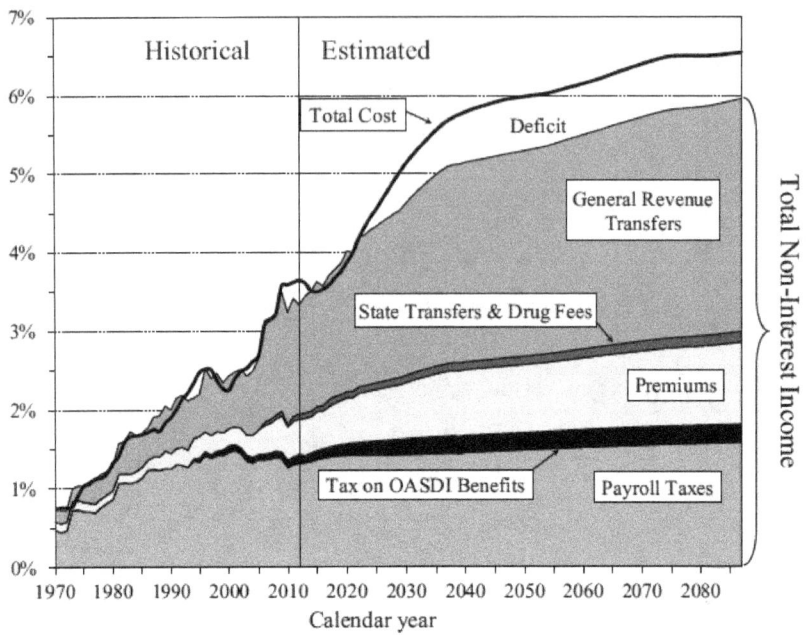

Projected revenue from payroll taxes and taxes on OASDI benefits credited to the HI Trust Fund increases from 1.4 percent of GDP in 2013 to 1.8 percent in 2087 under current law, while projected general revenue transfers to the SMI Trust Fund increase from 1.5 percent of GDP in 2013 to 2.9 percent in 2087, and beneficiary premiums increase from 0.5 to 1.0 percent of GDP. The share of total non-interest Medicare income from taxes falls substantially (from 41 percent to 30 percent) while general revenue transfers rises (from 43 to 50 percent), as does the share of premiums (from 14 percent to 17 percent). The distribution of financing changes in part because in Parts B and D—the Medicare components that are financed largely from general revenues—costs increase at a faster rate than Part A cost under the Trustees' projections. By 2087, the Medicare SMI program will require general revenue transfers equal to 2.9 percent of GDP. Moreover, the HI deficit represents a further 0.7 percent of GDP in 2087. There is no provision under current law to finance this deficit through general revenue transfers or any other revenue source.

The Medicare Modernization Act (2003) requires that the Board of Trustees determine each year whether the annual difference between program cost and dedicated revenues (the bottom four layers of Chart C) exceeds 45 percent of total Medicare cost in any of the first seven fiscal years of the 75-year projection period. In that case, the annual Trustees Report must include a determination of "excess general revenue Medicare funding." Two consecutive reports with such a determination triggers a "Medicare funding warning." The warning directs the President to submit proposed legislation within 15 days of the next budget submission to respond to the warning and requires Congress to consider the proposal on an expedited basis. To date, elected officials have not enacted legislation responding to these funding warnings which have been included in the six previous reports.

This year's report shows the difference between cost and dedicated financing revenues to exceed 45 percent of total Medicare cost during fiscal year 2013, prompting a determination of "excess general revenue Medicare funding," triggering another "Medicare funding warning" for the seventh consecutive year.

What are the Budgetary Implications of Rising Social Security and Medicare Costs? Concern about the long-range financial outlook for Medicare and Social Security often focuses on the depletion dates for the HI and OASDI trust funds—the times when the projected trust fund balances under current law will be insufficient to pay the full amounts of scheduled benefits. A more immediate issue is the effect the programs have on the unified Federal budget prior to depletion of the trust funds.

Chart D shows the excess of scheduled costs over dedicated tax and premium income for the OASDI, HI, and SMI trust funds expressed as percentages of GDP. Each of these trust funds' operations will contribute increasing amounts to Federal unified budget deficits in future years. General revenues pay for roughly 75 percent of all SMI costs. From now through 2026, interest earnings and asset redemptions, financed from general revenues, will cover the shortfall of HI tax and premium revenues relative to expenditures. In addition, general revenues must cover similar payments as a result of growing OASDI deficits through 2033.[1]

In 2013, the projected difference between Social Security's expenditures and dedicated tax income is $79 billion. For HI, the projected difference between expenditures and dedicated tax and premium income is $26 billion. The projected general revenue demands of SMI are $239 billion. Thus, the total General Fund requirements for Social Security and Medicare in 2013 are $344 billion, or 2.1 percent of GDP. Redemption of trust fund bonds, interest paid on those bonds, and transfers from the General Fund provide no new net income to the Treasury, which must finance these payments through some combination of increased taxation, reduc-

---

[1] As noted earlier in this summary, if trust fund depletion actually occurred as projected for HI in 2026 and for OASDI in 2033, each program could pay benefits thereafter only up to the amount of continuing dedicated revenues. Chart D, by contrast, compares dedicated sources of tax and premium income with the full cost of paying scheduled benefits under each program. In practice, lawmakers have never allowed the asset reserves of the Social Security or Medicare HI trust funds to become depleted.

tions in other government spending, or additional borrowing from the public.

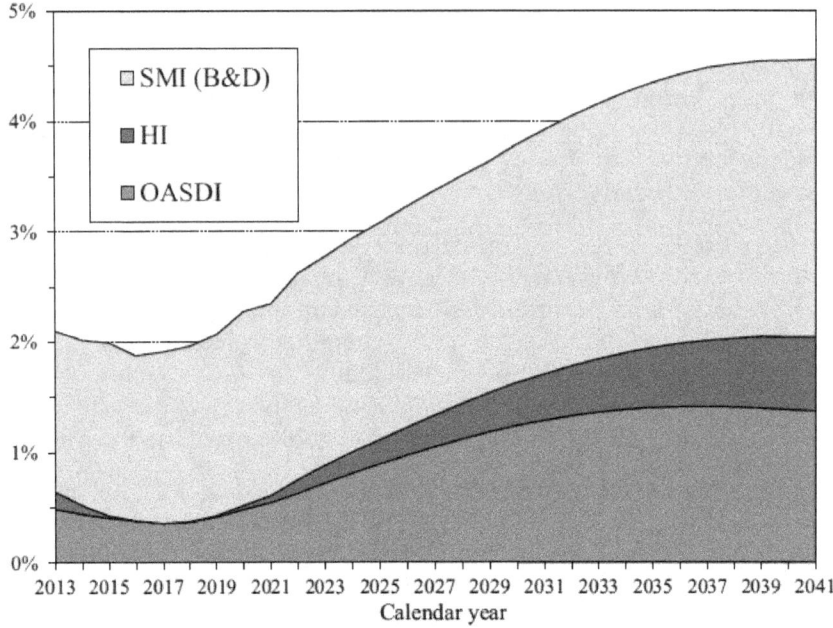

Chart D–Projected SMI General Revenue Funding plus OASDI and HI Tax Shortfalls
[Percentage of GDP]

Chart D shows that the difference between cost and revenue (expressed as a percentage of GDP) from dedicated payroll taxes, income taxation of benefits, and premiums will grow rapidly through the 2030s as the baby-boom generation reaches retirement age. This imbalance would result in vastly increased pressure on the Federal budget if the law were changed to maintain scheduled benefits in the absence of an increase in dedicated tax revenues, with such financing requirements equaling 4.5 percent of GDP by 2040.

What Is the Outlook for Short-Term Trust Fund Adequacy? The reports measure the short-range adequacy of the OASI, DI, and HI Trust Funds by comparing fund asset reserves to projected costs for the ensuing year (the "trust fund ratio"). A trust fund ratio of 100 percent or more—that is, asset reserves at least equal to projected cost for the next year—is a good indicator of a fund's short-range adequacy. That level of projected reserves for any year suggests that even if cost exceeds income, the trust fund reserves, combined with annual tax revenues, would be sufficient to pay full benefits for several years.

By this measure, the OASI Trust Fund is financially adequate throughout the 2013-22 period, but the DI Trust Fund fails the short-range test because its trust fund ratio was 85 percent at the beginning of 2013, with projected depletion of all reserves in 2016.

The HI Trust Fund also does not meet the short-range test of financial adequacy; its trust fund ratio was 81 percent at the beginning of 2013 based on the year's anticipated expenditures, and the projected ratio does not rise to 100 percent within five years. Projected HI Trust Fund asset reserves become fully depleted in 2026. Chart E shows the trust fund ratios through 2040 under the intermediate assumptions.

Chart E–OASI, DI, and HI Trust Fund Ratios
[Asset reserves as a percentage of annual cost]

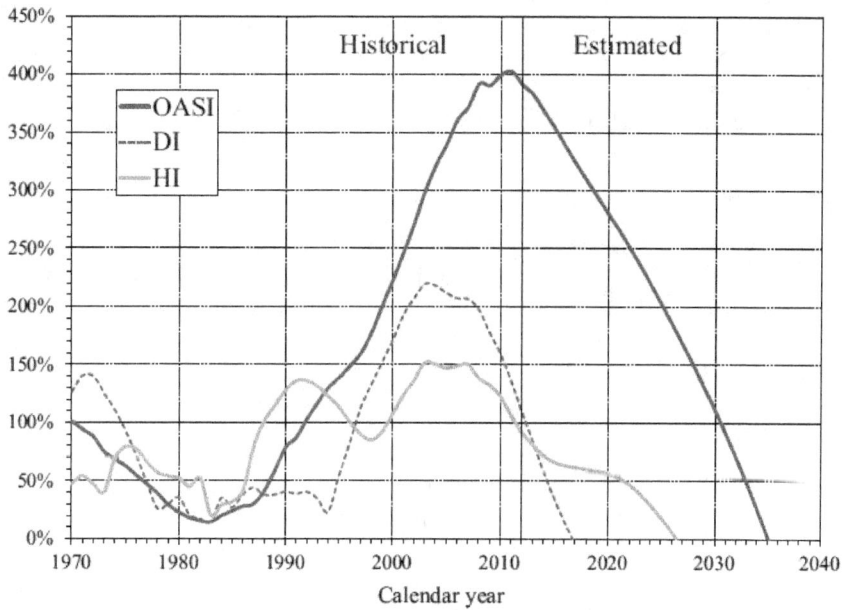

The Trustees apply a less stringent annual "contingency reserve" test to SMI Part B asset reserves because the overwhelming portion of the financing for that account consists of beneficiary premiums and general revenue contributions that are set each year to meet expected costs. Part D premiums paid by enrollees and the amounts apportioned from the General Fund of the Treasury are determined each year. Moreover, flexible appropriation authority established by lawmakers for Part D allows additional General Fund financing if costs are higher than anticipated, thereby eliminating the need for a contingency reserve in that account. Note, however, that estimated Part B costs are improbably low for 2014 and beyond because the projections assume that current law, which substantially reduces physician payments per service under the sustainable growth rate system, will not change. The estimated physician fee reduction for 2014 is 24.7 percent. A reduction in fees of this magnitude is highly unlikely; lawmakers have acted to prevent similar reductions in every year since 2003. Underestimated payments to physicians would affect projected costs for Part B, total SMI, and total Medicare.

What Are Key Dates in DI, OASI, and HI Financing? The 2013 reports project that the DI, OASI, and HI Trust Funds will all be depleted within the next 25 years. The following table shows key dates for the respective trust funds.

KEY DATES FOR THE TRUST FUNDS

	OASI	DI	OASDI	HI
Year of peak trust fund ratio[a]	2011	2003	2008	2003
First year cost exceeds income excluding interest[b]	2010	2005	2010	2018
First year cost exceeds income including interest[b].	2022	2009	2021	2021
Year trust fund reserves are depleted	2035	2016	2033	2026

[a] Dates pertain to the post-2000 period.

[b] Dates indicate the first year that a condition is projected to occur and to persist annually thereafter through 2087.

DI Trust Fund asset reserves, which have been declining since 2008, are projected to be fully depleted in 2016, as reported last year. Payment of full DI benefits beyond 2016, when tax income would cover only 80 percent of scheduled benefits, will require legislation to address the financial imbalance, possibly including a reallocation of the OASDI payroll tax rate between OASI and DI.

The OASI Trust Fund, when considered separately, has a projected reserves depletion date of 2035, unchanged from last year's report.

The combined OASDI trust funds have a projected depletion date of 2033, also unchanged from last year's report. After the depletion of reserves, continuing tax income would be sufficient to pay 77 percent of scheduled benefits in 2033 and 72 percent in 2087.

The OASDI reserves currently continue to grow because projected interest earnings ($103 billion in 2013) still substantially exceed the non-interest income deficit. This year's report indicates that annual OASDI income, including payments of interest to the trust funds from the General Fund, will exceed annual cost every year until 2021, increasing the nominal value of combined OASDI trust fund asset reserves. The trust fund ratio (the ratio of projected reserves to annual cost) will continue to decline gradually, as it has since 2008, despite this nominal balance increase. Beginning in 2021, net redemptions of trust fund asset reserves with General Fund payments will be required until projected depletion of these reserves in 2033.

The projected HI Trust Fund depletion date is 2026, two years later than reported last year. Under current law, scheduled HI tax and premium income would be sufficient to pay 87 percent of estimated HI cost in 2026 and 73 percent by 2087.

This report anticipates that in 2013 the HI Trust Fund's non-interest income deficit ($31 billion) will exceed projected interest earnings ($9 billion), requiring the use of $22 billion in asset reserves. Non-interest income is projected to exceed cost for 2015 through 2020 as the economic recovery continues, followed by increasing annual shortfalls of non-interest income through the remainder of the long-range projection period.

What is the Long-Range Actuarial Balance of the OASI, DI, and HI Trust Funds? Another way to view the outlook for payroll tax-financed trust funds is to consider their actuarial balances for the 75-year valuation period. The actuarial balance measure includes the trust fund asset reserves at the beginning of the period and all costs and income during the valuation period, all expressed as a percentage of taxable payroll for the 75-year projection period. Premium increases and general revenue transfers necessary to bring SMI into annual balance occur as a requirement of Federal law so actuarial balance is not an informative concept for that program.

The actuarial deficit represents the average amount of change in income or cost that is needed throughout the valuation period in order to achieve actuarial balance. The actuarial balance equals zero if cost for the period can be met for the period as a whole and trust fund asset reserves at the end of the period are equal to the following year's cost. The OASI, DI, and HI Trust Funds all have long-range actuarial deficits under the intermediate assumptions, as shown in the following table.

LONG-RANGE ACTUARIAL DEFICIT OF THE OASI, DI, AND HI TRUST FUNDS
[Percent of taxable payroll]

	OASI	DI	OASDI	HI
Actuarial Deficit................	2.40	0.32	2.72	1.11

The Trustees project that Social Security's annual deficits, expressed as the difference between the cost rate and income rate for a particular year, will decline from 1.26 percent of taxable payroll in 2013 to 0.98 percent in 2018 before increasing steadily to 3.87 percent in 2037. Annual deficits then decline slightly through 2050 before resuming an upward trajectory and reaching 4.77 percent in 2087 (Chart B). Increasing annual deficits during the final three decades of the projection indicate that a single tax rate increase for all years starting in 2013 sufficient to achieve actuarial balance would result in large annual surpluses early in the period followed by increasing deficits in later years. The relatively large deficits at the end of the 75-year projection period—equal to 4.77 percent of taxable payroll in 2087 (see Chart B discussion)—indicate that sustained solvency would require payroll tax rate increases or benefit reductions (or a combination thereof) by the end of the period that are substantially larger than those needed on average for this report's long-range period (2013-87).

Projected HI tax-income deficits (0.35 percent of taxable payroll in 2013) gradually decline to become a slight surplus in 2017 before deficits re-emerge to grow each year, reaching 1.58 percent of taxable payroll in 2048, after which the deficits remain in the 1.50 to 1.70 percent range through 2087.

The financial outlooks for both OASDI and HI depend on a number of demographic and economic assumptions. Nevertheless, the actuarial deficit in each of these programs is large enough that averting trust fund depletion under current-law financing is extremely unlikely. An analysis that allows plausible random variations around the intermediate assumptions employed in the report indicates that OASDI trust fund depletion is highly probable by mid-century.

How Has the Financial Outlook for Social Security and Medicare Changed Since Last Year? Under the intermediate assumptions, the combined OASDI trust funds have a projected 75-year actuarial deficit equal to 2.72 percent of taxable payroll, 0.05 percentage point larger than last year's estimate. The anticipated asset reserves depletion date remains 2033. The actuarial deficit increased by about 0.06 percent of payroll solely due to advancing the valuation date by one year and including the year 2087. The effects of recently enacted legislation, updated demographic data and assumptions, and updated economic data and assumptions worsened the actuarial deficit, but these effects were offset by updated programmatic data and improved methodologies, causing little additional change in the actuarial deficit.

Medicare's HI Trust Fund has a long-range actuarial deficit equal to 1.11 percent of taxable payroll under the intermediate assumptions, 0.24 percentage point smaller than reported last year. The lower Medicare cost projections are primarily due to favorable changes in provider assumptions based on recent data (for example, lower skilled nursing facility utilization and case mix increases for the next several years, and lower Medicare Advantage plan bid assumptions) and reduced HI expenditures experienced in the projection base year (2012). The projected date of depletion of the HI Trust Fund is now 2026, two years later than reported last year.

Who Are the Trustees? There are six Trustees, four of whom serve by virtue of their positions in the Federal Government: the Secretary of the Treasury, the Secretary of Labor, the Secretary of Health and Human Services, and the Commissioner of Social Security. The other two Trustees are public representatives appointed by the President and confirmed by the Senate: Charles P. Blahous III, Research Fellow at the Hoover Institution and Senior Research Fellow at the Mercatus Center, and Robert D. Reischauer, President Emeritus and Distinguished Fellow of the Urban Institute.

How Are Social Security and Medicare Financed? For OASDI and HI, the major source of financing is payroll taxes on earnings paid by employees and their employers. Self-employed workers pay the equivalent of the combined employer and employee tax rates. During 2012, an estimated 161 million people had earnings covered by Social Security and paid payroll taxes; for Medicare the corresponding figure was 165 million. Current law establishes payroll tax rates for OASDI, which apply to earnings up to an annual maximum ($113,700 in 2013) that ordinarily increases with the growth in the nationwide average wage. In contrast to OASDI, covered workers pay HI taxes on total earnings. The scheduled payroll tax rates (in percent) for 2013 are:

	OASI	DI	OASDI	HI	Total
Employees	5.30	0.90	6.20	1.45	7.65
Employers	5.30	0.90	6.20	1.45	7.65
Combined total. . .	10.60	1.80	12.40	2.90	15.30

Note that starting in 2013, the Affordable Care Act applies an additional HI tax equal to 0.9 percent of earnings over $200,000 for individual tax return filers, and on earnings over $250,000 for joint return filers.

Payments from the General Fund currently finance about 75 percent of SMI Part B and Part D costs, with most of the remaining costs covered by monthly premiums charged to enrollees or in the case of low-income beneficiaries, paid on their behalf by Medicaid for Part B and Medicare for Part D. Part B and Part D premium amounts are determined by methods defined in law and increase as the estimated costs of those programs rise.

In 2013, the Part B standard monthly premium is $104.90. There are also income-related premium surcharges for Part B beneficiaries whose modified adjusted gross income exceeds a specified threshold. In 2013 through 2019, the threshold is $85,000 for individual tax return filers and $170,000 for joint return filers. Income-related premiums range from $146.90 to $335.70 per month in 2013.

In 2013, the Part D "base monthly premium" is $31.17. Actual premium amounts charged to Part D beneficiaries depend on the specific plan they have selected and average around $30 for standard coverage. Part D enrollees with incomes exceeding the thresholds established for Part B must pay income-related monthly adjustment amounts in addition to their normal plan premium. For 2013, the adjustments range from $11.60 to

$66.60 per month. Part D also receives payments from States that partially compensate for the Federal assumption of Medicaid responsibilities for prescription drug costs for individuals eligible for both Medicare and Medicaid. In 2013, State payments will cover about 12 percent of Part D costs.

A MESSAGE FROM THE PUBLIC TRUSTEES

These are the third annual reports in which we have participated as Public Trustees. As with our experiences preparing the prior years' reports, we were once again impressed by the quality and professionalism of the work performed by the actuaries' offices in the Social Security Administration and the Centers for Medicare and Medicaid Services, and by all of the staff dedicated by the departments of the ex officio Trustees. We believe the public continues to be well served by the statutory process for developing the financial projections for Social Security and Medicare. Though only the passage of time will reveal the degree of accuracy in our projections, we are pleased to vouch for the objectivity and integrity of the Trustees' estimation process.

Both the Social Security and Medicare programs face substantial financing shortfalls that require legislative corrections, but the implications are different for each one. Of the two programs, Social Security faces the larger actuarial imbalance as well as the most immediate threat of trust fund depletion, again projected in 2016 for its Disability Insurance (DI) Trust Fund. Accordingly, more far-reaching legislative measures are required to maintain the solvency of Social Security relative to Medicare. On the other hand, Medicare is projected to experience relatively greater cost growth over the long-range valuation period, posing greater strains for the federal budget as a whole due to the extent to which its financing depends on general revenues. The legislative measures required to maintain Medicare solvency are not as pronounced as they are for Social Security, but Medicare still requires substantial further reforms if it is not to eventually subject the general budget to severe levels of strain.

Chart A in our report summary illustrates how, relative to GDP, both Social Security and Medicare costs increased sharply in recent years, largely as a consequence of the Great Recession. The economic recovery will cause costs for both programs relative to GDP to level off during the middle of this decade. But as Chart A also shows, both programs are poised to resume a rapid pace of annual cost growth by the end of this decade.

Social Security's long-term income shortfall is now larger than it has been at any point since before the landmark program reforms of 1983. The dates of projected depletion of each of its trust funds are unchanged from last year's report. It is important to grasp that the amount of time remaining to enact a financing solution that is both reasonably balanced and politically plausible is far less than the amount of time projected before final depletion of Social Security's combined trust funds. Toward that end, this year's report contains new illustrations of the magnitudes of benefit changes required if lawmakers wish to preserve solvency without affecting current beneficiaries. Importantly, even if a Social Security solution were enacted today and effective immediately, it would require financing corrections that are substantially more severe than those enacted in the 1983 program amendments. Each passing year of legislative inaction reduces the likelihood that a solution can be found that is acceptable to lawmakers on both sides of the political aisle.

As Table IV.B7 of the Social Security Trustees Report shows, those now entering the Social Security system as workers will contribute more in taxes (in present value) than they receive in benefits under current schedules. The entirety of Social Security's financing shortfall thus consists of an excess of scheduled benefits over taxes contributed for current and past program participants. This information highlights the importance, from an equity perspective, of enacting a solution promptly enough so that more generations contribute to correcting the program's financing shortfall. Substantial further delay risks further concentrating the burdens of correcting the shortfall on the younger workers who already stand to be treated less favorably, thereby undermining Social Security's efficacy in serving future generations.

As lawmakers contemplate solutions to Social Security's shortfall, we commend the information published by the Social Security Chief Actuary's office at:
www.ssa.gov/OACT/solvency/index.html, *and*
www.ssa.gov/OACT/solvency/provisions/index.html.
These links provide access to the SSA Chief Actuary's analyses of individual provisions as well as comprehensive proposals for addressing program financing.

Because the primary focus is on the revenues and benefit costs associated with current law, this year's Medicare Trustees Report contains fewer references to the alternative scenarios in which certain cost-saving provisions of the 2010 Affordable Care Act are assumed to be overridden. Readers who want additional information about the illustrative alternative fiscal scenario can find it at:
www.cms.gov/Research-Statistics-Data-and-Systems/Statistics-Trends-and-Reports/ReportsTrustFunds/Downloads/2013TRAlternativeScenario.pdf.

As with Social Security, we recommend that legislative measures be enacted to close the Medicare Hospital Insurance (HI) financing shortfall, and to reduce projected cost growth in its SMI components of Parts B and D. But to a greater extent than Social Security, the Medicare projections also depend on the course of new technology and whether various revenue and cost-reduction measures scheduled to be phased in over the next several years are successfully implemented. It is important for Medicare finances that these measures not be scaled back or repealed without replacing them with others that produce an equal or greater amount of cost savings.

The durability of the Social Security and Medicare programs through the decades rests in large part on public perceptions that their methods of financing, while not perfect, are generally fair. While considerations of equity and adequacy will inevitably accompany any legislative effort to restore these programs to long-term financial balance, a broadly accepted solution becomes less likely the longer that financing corrections are postponed. In the interests of those who depend on these programs as beneficiaries, as well as those who contribute to them as taxpayers, we urge lawmakers to correct the financial imbalances of Social Security and Medicare soon.

CHARLES P. BLAHOUS III,
Trustee.

ROBERT D. REISCHAUER,
Trustee.

2013

www.ingramcontent.com/pod-product-compliance
Lightning Source LLC
Chambersburg PA
CBHW070845310526
45793CB00011B/593